If This is How You Love

POEMS BY KAYLA KENNEDY

IF THIS IS HOW YOU LOVE

www.thekennedyluck.com

ISBN: 978-0-578-33620-6

First edition: January 2022

Illustrations and cover design by Ronald Beek III

Dedication

I would be lying, if I dedicated this book to anyone other than my own damn heart, that fickle bastard.

But I would be remiss, if I did not dedicate this heart to Eric, the one who stayed.

Contents

How you love your family

They say blood is thicker than water.
Yet again, they have erased history.

As the proverb goes,
"The blood of the covenant is thicker than the water
of the womb."

And I choose you.

If This is How You Love

You're standing in front of me and you say,
"I love my kids. You have to believe me.
I really do love my kids."
And I think to myself,
then why do you do this to them?
Why are we here?

Love does not sound like
a call from your daughter on a Saturday afternoon
telling us no one has been home in three days,
and they ran out of food,
and her brother is crying,
and she doesn't know what to do.

It does not look like
an infestation of ants marching
over the littered pile of trash on your kitchen counters,
or the string of men
rotating through your bedroom door
like a merry go-round,
bearing their horse teeth and taking you for a ride,
while you hum a tune of cotton candy bliss.

It does not look like
the ride in the back of an ambulance,
while strangers in uniforms give you Narcan
for the second time,
or your youngest son
found alone in a crack house.

Love is not shaded with the color of bruises
hidden beneath cotton tee shirts.
It does not smell like piss in the fridge
and beer on the carpet.

It does not taste like iron,
like crusted blood on the lower lip.
And it certainly does not sound like
the empty sobs echoing from your chest,
as you stand in front of me
claiming to know what love looks like.

But I don't say any of this.
I simply reply, "I know."
Because I am not a firefly
able to make light where there is none.
And after all this clamoring in the dark,
my heart is too heavy with all the reasons to hate you.
I am too tired to give you a poem
when there is nothing poetic about it.

I want to feel sorry for you.
Maybe you are telling the truth.
Perhaps, love does not just infect the strong,
but haunts even the weakest of us.
It does not discriminate
the way that hate does.
And who am I to call you a liar
for not being strong enough?

But then I look at him,
this little boy who climbs into stranger's laps
and says "I love you"
because he doesn't know any better,
because you never taught him
what it really feels like,
because he's been in a proverbial field
chasing fireflies,
when he deserves the whole goddamn sun,
and I can't.

So, if this is how you love, then don't.

Uncle moon

Phase 1.

The first lie you ever told me,
we were sitting at my mother's kitchen table.
It was nineteen-ninety-something,
and I imagined that we were the council
of the sun and the moon
because I ruled over the day
and you were always out at night.

"Uncle moon?" I asked.
You replied, "Yes, my little sun?"
"Tell me about the kingdom of the night."

And with a half-crescent-Chesire-cat smile
you spun a wonderland story
of the creatures who played
on the dark side of the moon.
I didn't know then
that the dark side was a myth,
and the creature who lived there was
simply a man
who couldn't find the light,
even when it was sitting right in front of him.

You pointed to the sky and told me
that the moon was always there,
even during the day.
You forgot to mention that 'always there'
meant 239,000 miles away,
far enough to disappear
but strong enough to push and pull the tides
without ever being hit by a wave.

You once told my mother
you would've become a very different man
if only she had chosen you instead of my father.
How different your life could've turned out.

But when you held me as an infant,
you dropped me on my head,
twice.

We joke that the first time was an accident
and the second was to set me right again.
But now I wonder if I was like your life,

a bar of soap
you tried desperately to hold onto
as it slipped through your fingers
and if only you could grasp it,

it would make you clean.

Phase III.

When you had a child of your own,
you held that baby in your arms and promised him
that you would learn to shine like the sun,
but you didn't know how.

So, we gave you the newspaper
and the glue,
and scissors,
and told you how to make one,

because not all sons are made of stars.
I handed you paint as golden as the lies you told,
said it might be messy
but it will get the job done.

Then you built a fire
from your papier-mache wings
and cried when it melted,
and I grow weary of your Icarus tale.

Phase IV.

Sometimes I feel sorry for you
and the sad, broken man you have become.
But your ghostly face
and melted wax wings

won't make up for what you did
or more importantly,
what you didn't do.
I am tired

of your crocodile tears,
and your crater sized pockmarked promises.
I no longer believe
your mad hatter excuses

and march hare lies.
Because our fingers are bloody and bruised
from your waning feather made words
and that boy

might spend the rest of his life thinking
that nobody wanted him.
And it is all your fault.
I should've known

that you will always be the moon.

Fruit of the poisonous tree

My father tried
to heal the wounds of his brother
in the shape of you,
but it cut his heart.
The venom seeped into his pores,
melted his bones like acid,
and molded him into an uglier version of himself,
like a wick burned and frayed,
like a tortoise morphed into a snapping turtle.

My mother tried to hold you
but it coiled around her limbs,
constricted her ribcage until it cracked,
siphoned every last breath from her collapsed lungs,
until there was nothing left
but bitterness and anger and regret
squeezed too tight like her pre-baby jeans
or a tired Raggedy Ann doll.

You crave attention
the way your mother craved the pipe,
racing and insatiable,
and my Narcan is empty.

I have nothing to give you
but the snake that bit my father
and suffocated my mother.
Maybe disappointment is hereditary.

Maybe failure poisons the tree like a plague
passed from one generation to the next.
Maybe it's in our genes
to whisper I love you
when we meant to say goodbye.

I think it's called poetic irony

I found myself burning apologies in my hands
like unsteady candles,
and handing them out to villains,
to keep them warm.

Then wondering why
they chose to burn the world with them instead.
Then my mother,
the same woman who branded me

with her own Irish Catholic sarcasm,
you know
the kind that drips with acid guilt,
turned to me and said,

"Well, that's because
you are more understanding than me.
More understanding than most people."

And it's funny because, well,
because it seems so *understanding* of her.

Tire swing: part one

There is a tree in my parent's backyard
with a tire swing hanging from one of the branches.

I remember when my father hung it there.
He took a fraying rope
and flung it carelessly into the air
hoping
it would sling itself over the strongest branch
and fall on the other side, so he could tie a knot.

But he missed.
Instead, it wrapped itself around a weaker branch
so many times, it got stuck.
No matter how he pulled and tugged
it would not come back down.

So, in true father fashion,
he looped it through the tire and made a swing anyway.
It was precarious, for sure, unsafe even,
but it was the nineties.

No matter how much our mother begged us not to,
warned us that branch would snap any day now,
told us not to test our luck,
we did it anyway.

Every day, every summer, again and again,
wondering
if today would be the day it finally gave out.
With one foot on the rubber,
two hands on the rope,
and nothing to catch our fall,
we swung,
soared through the air,
praying

that this time it would still want to hold our weight,
that this time the rope would not break
and send us hurtling to the ground,
that this time would not be the last time.

It has been more than twenty years
and the tire swing is still there,
still fraying,
still just one swing away from snapping.

We are all grown up now
and just a little too scared
to go one more time,
to be the one who finally breaks it.

And I think, maybe, this is what love feels like.

How you love in all the wrong places

Tire swing: part two

We take our fraying hearts
and fling them carelessly at love,
hoping
to find *the* one.

But we miss.
Instead, it wraps itself around the *wrong* one
so many times, it gets stuck.
No matter how much it begs us not to,
warns us it will snap any day now,
tells us not to test our luck,
we do it anyway.

Each time, again and again,
wondering
if today will be the day it finally gives out.
We fall toward love with nothing to catch us,
we swing,
soar through the air,
praying,

that this time it will hold our weight,
that this time it will not break us,
that this time will not be the last time.

It has been more than twenty years
and my heart is still there,
still fraying,
still just one swing away from snapping.
But we are all grown up now
and just a little too scared
to go one more time,
to be the one who finally breaks it.

And I think, maybe, this is what memory feels like.

The first time I heard it I was a martyr

He told me that he loved me
and I felt robbed.
Because it was the first boy that had ever said it to me,
and he didn't mean it.
He couldn't mean it.

And when I told him that I didn't love him back,
he told me that I "would grow to"
as if love was something he could teach me.
But that didn't sound right.
It couldn't be right.

And when I told him that I just wanted to be friends,
he told me just "how hard it was to be around" me
sometimes,
as if that was supposed to make me feel bad.
Which it did,

because I didn't know how to keep him safe in the space
of our friendship.
And when I told him so,
he said, "Stop being a fucking martyr."
And to this day,

I still don't know what I was supposed to say.
Because he was asking me to worship
at an altar he did not have,
and wait for a god to answer.
So, isn't a martyr what he was looking for all along?

Muse

How many times have I looked at my body
and wished it were made of clay?
To be sculpted into perfection
by hands that loved me into being

But now,
your love is a stained-glass memory
painted on every panel of my skin,
shaded from the bruises you made them with,

and I don't want to be your muse anymore.

Landmine syllables

He was the first person
to show me the power of words.
How an artillery of consonants
can you leave you bleeding.

How a string of vowels
can shield the pain.
And how sometimes,
they come from the canon.

I learned how
to tip-toe across the floor
so as not to cut my feet on broken eggshells.
How to craft my words very carefully,

to comb through sentences
in search of landmine syllables
the ones you never thought to look for
but would explode all the same.

Alien

Try and convince me that you could love only one star.
Convince me with your pleasant, sugary smile
and doe-eyed hopeful heartbeat.
Convince me with the honeyed lilt to your voice,
and the wit on your tongue,
and the SAT word you just learned.

Look at me the way fire looks at rain,
just begging to be put out.
And I'll wish I was in love with you instead of the sky.
And I'll want to *want* to go home with you.
But I'm not the rain you think I am.

You see, that's the flaw with us
glimmering-stardust-dreamers.
We luminescent, radiant beings of fractured light.
We are in fact fractured,
splintered into organs,
ruptured into conscious thought,
congested into flesh and bone.
We look up at the night sky
and we see two different things.
You see me and how we were born to shine.
I see you and the black space around the stars.
Neither existing without the other,
but fragmented for all time.

You want me to swallow you whole.
But all the frat houses, and speakers,
and liquid courage in the world can't do that.
And that's why I'm the alien.
Because you're over there
stridently trying to fall in love with me.
And I'm over here,
silently in love with a broken sky.

Gone

Some days I wished you were gone
and then one day you were.

And the emptiness inside me grew so big
it leaked out until there was nothing left.

Now I wonder about the contradictions.
How can emptiness bleed?
How can we be full of nothing?

Butterflies

I get butterflies in my stomach
when I look at you.

Butterflies: also known as
conspicuous creatures of love and beauty.
Symptoms include:
Flittering nausea,
fluttering heartbeat,
sweaty palms
and a warm gooey center,
vibrant fiery warfare
coursing through every muscle of your body,
and a voice so cocooned
that when your ruminating thoughts
finally crystalize themselves into flighty words,
squirm their way up your throat
and through your lips,
they hover in the air and
die.

Butterflies: also known as
monsters.
Symptoms include:
Monstrous rebirth where
your skin splits open,
your soul climbs out,
expands its wings to dry and then just
flies away.

You are beautiful like a butterfly,
the way a star fuses and collapses when it is born,
the way it explodes when it dies,
like blistering summer love
or a glass menagerie,
fleeting and bittersweet.

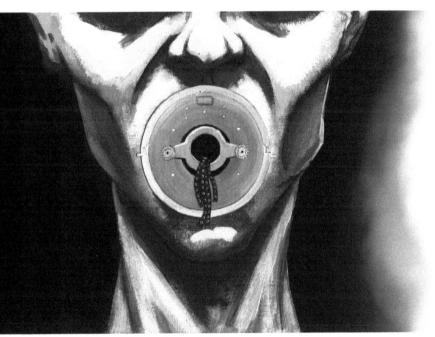

How you love the one who left

The one who left said

"I don't need you. I want you."

I want you, he said.
I want you.
And I believed him.

The tragedy is,
I think he believed it too.

And I knew that people let you go
when they don't need you anymore.
But I didn't know
they could just stop wanting you.

Love letters

Your lips block the words that try to escape.
The ones that my heart had whispered too faint.
Neurons are sent from my brain but they die,
synapses fizzling as your skin touches mine.

I wish I could take the words that you say,
write them all down and send them your way.
Postmarked with a stamp and my name
scrawled in ink at the end of the page.

I want you.
I want you.
I want you so bad.

Spills from your mouth and it's driving me mad.
And I want so badly to tell you the same,
but I can't for fear of losing the game
A tired "me too" just isn't right.

But I can't find the words by the end of the night.
So, I clutch at your shirt and the hem of your jeans,
Pull you in close,
and hope you get what I mean.

The second time I heard it - I was a fool

We were both a little drunk. It was a long day. I could
count down the days to graduation.

That's when he said it.
"I couldn't stop staring at you. It really hit me; you're
leaving."
"Are you crying?"
I asked him.

"No, shut up."

"You are, why are you crying?
I'm supposed to be the one crying.
It's going to be ok."

"No, it's not."
"Why?"

"Because I think I love you."
"You what?"

"I love you."

I panicked for a second.
I'm pretty sure all normal bodily functions were paralyzed.
I told him,
"You're only saying that
because you're drunk,
and you'll change your mind in the morning."

"No,
I've been thinking it for days, I really have.
I tried to tell you, but I couldn't."

Then I started to cry, not the pretty kind of silent tears, but
a blubbering mess with snot leaking out the nose.
"I think I might just love you too."

I wanted this. I asked for it.
But only fools dream of reaching the other side of love
just because they want to know what a heart sounds like
when it breaks.

29

On this Ledge

We fell in love the way a ledge hugs a mountain.
You warned me to tread lightly
as I flattened every inch of myself against your skin,
but I didn't listen.

I climbed into your arms
and made a home there,
even as you told me you were crumbling.
I fell in love,

as if it alone could save me,
even as you begged me not to.
So now, we are stuck, frozen in place,
because I can't move, and you can't seem to leave.

We are two wary adventurers,
holding on to something so precarious,
so wildly dangerous,
that to slip is to end everything,

and who are we without each other?
You don't need me
in the same way that I need you,
but neither of us are strong enough to let go.

You can't help but give me this breadth of stone,
and I can't help but cling to the edge of you
and brace myself for the fall.
As if it could hurt any more

than on this ledge.

Sea glass

You told me how you were a broken bottle
on shores end,
so afraid that I would cut myself against you,
and I was a rising tide,
threatening to pull you in closer.

You said we would roll and tumble together
until I spit you back out,
worn thin and smooth
and safe enough,
for someone else's hands.

Said you would love me,
but an ocean only crashes
against the sand,
said I would lose you.

But all I saw
waiting in the blue of your eyes
was sea-glass.
And I thought, how beautiful,
this weathered thing,
this fractured, shattered soul made art,
this littered glass shaped by the sea
into something new and wanted.
Pretty enough to hang in windows
or wear around your neck.
Something people search for and collect.
And I wish I had listened.

Because the thing about glass is
it breaks.
And even rock wears away.
And sometimes people tell the truth,
if you let them.

Hold on

To let go,
is to suffocate.
If we can just hold on
long enough,
we will never have to breathe
air again.

"You don't love me anymore, do you?"

"Honestly, no I don't."

Well, that hurt

Iron lung

I should regret you.
At least, that's what everyone keeps telling me.
I should be angry.
But what do I have to be truly angry about?

That we ran out of time?
We never had it from the start.
Or perhaps, because
you once clung to me as if I were your only breath,

my lips your iron lung,
expanding and contracting
with the rise and fall of your chest.
Until one day, you could breathe on your own

and you didn't need me anymore.
You once brought me such joy that I refuse to regret it.
I will never understand
how the boy who made me believe I was whole

could be so broken.
One day, we gave each other the reflections
we could not see for ourselves.
How can I possibly be angry about that?

How you love yourself

The wardrobe

My confidence is just like a dress I wear,
slipped on in the morning
and slipped back off at night.

Pride is
heavy,
but "she wears it well".

It's feeling flawless
after the tenth outfit you've tried on.

It's going to work without any makeup on
and telling them you are sick
when they ask how you feel,
because it is better to be sick
than to be ugly.

Pride is
a painted smile beneath the mask of zorro.

It is five months of silence.

It is blaming your anxiety when you tell me
you do not love me anymore.

A moment on the lips, a lifetime on the hips

She should feel beautiful.
At least, that's what they keep telling her.
If only the spirals of her self-doubt
would coil around her hips

as tightly and infinitely
as they do her thoughts,
then she would believe them.
But I know her.
I am her.

And I've spent a lifetime
trying to remember a moment
when the word "beautiful"

didn't feel like a lie on my tongue,
or an assault made by someone else's lips.

Bare bones

You should not worry so much.
At least, that's what everyone keeps telling you.
But anxiety does not care about privilege.
Even your alabaster skin cannot shield you
from the parasitic microbes
burrowed underneath its surface,
nestled into the marrow of your bones,
teeming, wriggling in every pore.
How can you be you?
When only one in every ten cells of the body
is actually human.

You should say how you feel,
they keep telling you.
But how do you say that you are too afraid
to be left alone
with the colonies of your Self?
That to love you,
is to love trillions of organisms that are not you.
There are less words in your throat
than there are bacteria.

So instead, you tell a pretty girl that you love her
and you do not mean it.
You sleep in the safety of her arms,
rest in the cavern of her collarbone.
Until one day, you realize you cannot stay.
Distance makes the air grow thinner
and you were already gasping before she got here.

Through the looking glass

The mirror is a clever thief.
I don't remember when it first stole from me.
When it broke in and carried away my confidence
without so much as a fingerprint on the doorframe,
or a footstep on the carpet.

I may not have even known it was there,
had it not left the door open on the way out.
An invitation for all the creatures lurking in the streets
who would slip in, one by one, when I wasn't looking.
I hardly noticed at first.

Shame hid in the basement.
She curled herself around the cables
behind the washing machine
where all the lost socks go.

Doubt hung from the rafters in the attic,
dripping slime over broken bike tires
and grade school trophies.

Anger snuck down the chimney,
a soot-covered criminal with a penchant for trouble.
He let the smoke in with no place to escape,
made it so hard to breathe.

Anxiety rattled in the closets.
Vanity painted herself across the tiles
on the bathroom floor.

I didn't know
I was sharing my home
with these crooks.

The mirror is a con artist.
Made me believe a refracted image of the truth,
a distorted perception reversed, bent, and broken,
disillusioned by a piece of glass,
reflecting not what it stole,
but what it gave back.

It took her, my confidence.
Dragged her away,
pressed against the concrete, beat,
cut at, until there was nothing left
but a ghost
loitering under the streetlamp,
waiting for someone to bring her home.

When I finally found her,
she asked why it took so long to come for her.

I named the mirror a culprit,
blamed the monsters it let in
for holding me hostage in my own skin,
but she didn't believe me.

Said even Alice made it back
through the looking glass.

I left the door unlocked.
I didn't even notice she was gone.

I left the lights on for my guests,
like moths to flame,
and the mirror had shown me
who was to blame.

Rusty pipes

I try to tell myself,
"You are beautiful."

But,
my voice is rust on an iron pipe.
It corrodes with every breath.

If I were a rose,

What if,
she had spit fire,
and grew thorns?

You plucked her
every last petal,
like a lovelorn schoolgirl.

But what if,
she hadn't smelled sweet
when you crushed her?

I would grow wild

What if that little girl
hadn't had the notion
that every broken soul needed her?
What if she were you, now?

Holding yourself to a promise
you made when you were six.
What if you hadn't lost yourself,
in all the people that needed you?

Or maybe it was just the one person
who needed you,
and used you,
and never had the courtesy to fully leave you.

and never ask for less.

I dream of a world
in which I do not ask my body to be less,
almost as much as
I ask my body to be less.

Less pimples
Less dark circles
Less stretch marks
Less fat

Less of me.
And although the mirror tells me
that it is too much,
I have never asked for more.

How you love the one who stayed

I have fallen in love with fictional characters so many times, I imagined that I would know what true love would feel like when I finally found it.

But I was wrong.

The one who stayed didn't say anything

He's tall.
That's usually the first thing people notice about him.
But the first thing I remember noticing about him,
was his silence.

Being a person who talks far too much,
and often far too long,
of course, I would notice that
he doesn't say a whole lot.

I'm a girl in love with words.
But if there's anything that love has taught me,
it's that pretty words can mean nothing
at all.

And now I'm falling in love with silence,
standing at an altar,
praying to a god I don't believe in,
that it doesn't slip away.

The third time I heard it I was in love

A little liquid courage,
and I'm pouring my heart out
and demanding that he tell me
if he feels the same way.

And then he's asking me to move in with him,
and I haven't the faintest memory
of how the conversation transitioned here.
And of course, I say yes.

But then I can't remember what he said before,
the part about loving me and all.
So, I make him say it again.
And of course, he does.

A poet in love

The average human heart has a resting rate
of 72 beats per minute.
That's about 3 billion heartbeats in a lifetime.
Yet, most days,
I can't hear a single one of them.
So I wonder, if maybe,
you can only hear your heart when it's breaking.

Like in a song, or a book, or poetry.
Poems are the fingerprints of rhythmic vessels,
an open cavity for a sequence in time repeated,
a metaphysical x-ray,
photographic evidence
of an otherwise invisible song,
and poets are organs
who sing when they bleed.

I want to say something true.
So, I open my mouth to speak,
but a metaphor falls out.
My throat is an open wound bleeding symphonies
of wine-red couplets and rose-colored verse.
I can make you a watercolor tragedy with painted tears.
I could write you an odyssey from an orchestra of pain.
I have so many words inside me,
I could drag razor blades across every inch of my skin,
and fill it with ink,
so that every time you touch me
your fingers stain black with my blood.

Heartbreak is a tattoo
that never fades from a poet's skin.
A violin is so much sweeter than a drumline.
That is why it is so hard for me to *just* tell you,
what it is that I want to tell you.

To speak plainly,
is to erase every line I have etched,
cut every chord I have sketched,
deafen the only melody I know how to play.
Without it, I'm afraid
I'll have nothing to say.

Maybe one day I'll be brave enough
to stand here and just tell you how I feel
without having to hide behind metaphors.
To say, I love you.
It is the truest thing that I know.

But a poet in love is like an amputee victim,
hands twitching over phantom keys,
mouth moving without any speech,
a stringless piece of harmony
reaching out for a broken limb
that has already healed.

We don't understand how to make words work.
How to make them stand alone
without a stanza to hold them,
the way that you hold me,
fearless and simple.
You breathe music without lyrics.
Your silence is a philharmonic concinnity,
It beats and I can hear everything.

Share with me the immortal ichor in your veins.
so that I may know love
the way you know the gods.
Now, I don't believe in God,
but I believe in you.
And if he does exist,
I bet he tastes like your lips,
and sounds just like this.

To the brave soul who dares love a poet

You will get love letters, a lot of them,
even though you didn't ask for them,
didn't even really want them in the first place.
But you will keep them,
in the drawer of your bedside table,
not because you'll ever read them again,
but because you know they mean something.
Even if you're not sure what that is, exactly.

You will be scared, at first, because you have heard
that a poet only writes about two things,
love and pain,
and too often they are the same thing.

A love letter from a poet is dangerous
It is open heart surgery,
the skeleton, all bare bones and rusty pipes,
an iron lung drowning in sea glass and butterflies.
It is 2001,
and you are too afraid to open the envelope because it
might be laced with anthrax, these words
might be laced with poison, with landmine syllables,
with all the hurt she has ever felt,
every unrequited look and empty promise,
every hollow touch and goodbye,
every single "I don't love you anymore"
and you will wish you could erase every line.
But you can't.

So, you keep them, because you love her.
Because she wrote them for you.
Because it makes her happy, to give these to you,
even if it is too heavy a gift for you to take.

The paper weighted by decades of heartbreak,
yearning and learning, for you, the final test,
your hands, the scales. It needed to be heavy
to make sure you could feel it,
and know that it was yours.

How far it travelled to reach you,
collecting stamps like badges of honor,
all wrinkled and bent, but still intact,
and ready to be opened, to be read by someone
more in love with the poet, than the pen.

She has been writing these letters to you
for a long, long time.
Before you'd ever met her.
Maybe that is why they are written in a language you do
not seem to understand.

Ancient and unmistakably foreign,
they speak of scars on skin that is not damaged
they paint confessions in which love is a crime,
and you are a cure, healing
something you don't believe to be broken.

Her words will equate you to the sun and the moon and
the stars. They will breathe life into every inch of you,
create whole worlds from you,
but forget, that you are only a man
and it costs you nothing to see her.
You do not need an explanation.
You do not need a whole book.

And you would tell her so,
but you are not a poet,
only the brave soul in love with one.

Star-crossed

When love found me, in the shape of you,
I hardly recognized it at first.

I was told that true love was a 90-mph roller coaster,
a beating heart one inch from death, racing,
reaching, breathless. That it would feel like
the beginning and end of everything.
That it might even hurt a little because that's what happens
when you fall, it hurts.
But it didn't.

Loving you has been as easy as breathing.
You are not the adventure, you are home.
That's what being with you feels like, like coming home.
Like finally opening your mouth after holding your breath
for twenty years.
Like stillness.

They say that newlyweds can't keep their hands off each
other, and maybe that's true. But not for all the reasons
they told me.
Not because we need to consume one another, lose
ourselves in a tangle of limbs, grasp at something you're
afraid will leave as soon as you let go.
No, it's a simple reminder that you are still here. Like the
ground when you've finished spinning in circles just to
watch the horizon blur.

You are here.
You are here.
You are here.

A kintsugi love

For Christmas he bought me a watch
to replace the one I broke.
It was even more beautiful than the first.

For our anniversary, he bought me a claddagh ring
to replace the one I lost,
the one my mother had given me.
And it was even more beautiful than the first.

Day by day, he kisses away the scars that came before,
and I wonder
if he will just keep replacing the lost and broken bits of me
with even more beautiful versions of myself.

Last year, he bought me a diamond
and promised forever.
It hasn't broken yet.
I haven't lost it either.

A miracle, I'm sure.
But even if I do, I'm not worried.
It's like that Japanese art, kintsugi,
and all the cracks are filled with him.

Epilogue

Follow me home

I miss when the moon would follow me home
and the stars were a map in the sky.
When digging a hole in the earth, in the yard,
meant you would come out on the other side.
When the bed was a ship, and the bath was a sea,
and the stairs were a mountain to climb.
When rangers and wizards, and pirates and treasure,
were always so easy to find.

I miss when the moon would follow me home
and the stars would get caught in your eyes.
When digging a hole in my heart, in my chest,
wasn't your morning goodbye.
When our bed was the ship, and your mouth was the sea,
and we swayed up and down with the tide.
When the pain and the lies, and the trail of my tears
were never so easy to find.

I miss when the moon would follow me home
and the stars wrote your name in the sky.
When digging a hole in the ground, in the yard,
wasn't our last goodbye.
When your bed wasn't laid with roses and weeds,
and the stairs were not too steep to climb.
When the wrinkles and years, and lines on my face,
were never so easy to find.

I miss when the moon would follow me home
instead of just lighting the sky.
When we were young, and free, and in love
and we hadn't run out of time.

Acknowledgements

Firstly, I would like to thank my parents, for teaching me never to accept less than what I deserve. Because of them, I have never had to live in a world where I did not feel loved. And my brother, who has, and always will be, my best friend.

Thank you to Ron, for adding technicolor to this black and white picture of mine. For your art, of course, but more importantly for your friendship.

To Meghan, for filling the passenger seat with a smile as I dragged you from one event to the next. For listening, and reading, and reminding me what it looks like to love yourself.

Lastly, to all my loves, both past and present. For teaching me how.

ABOUT THE AUTHOR

Kayla Kennedy is an avid reader, writer, actress, producer, and poet. She studied Criminal Justice, Psychology, and Theatre Arts at Westfield State University and received a master's degree in Applied Behavior Analysis from Simmons College.

Over the years, Kayla has dabbled in both the arts and sciences. As a Board-Certified Behavior Analyst, she works with families affected by autism and other social disabilities. As an artist, she finds herself engulfed in one project after the next. From founding a theatre company, *Spectrum Studios Theatre*, and running workshops, to poetry slams in Cambridge, to the airwaves, cohosting the *What's the Story Podcast* on the WTFAWTA network.

Born and raised in Massachusetts, she currently resides there with her husband and their 200-pound puppy. For more information on her latest ventures, please visit www.thekennedyluck.com

ABOUT THE ILLUSTRATOR

Ron Beek III is a lover of stories. This led
him to Montserrat College of Art in
Beverly Massachusetts. where he went
on to receive a BFA in Illustration with a
minor in creative writing. He has written
and illustrated several comic books
including *Glass Lake: Onto Others* and.
with frequent collaborator Ryan Alves. *The Punishment: Social Justice.*
He was a producer on the 2013 documentary *Legends of the Knight.*
about the positive impact Batman- his favorite character- has had on
the lives of people like himself. As a lifelong film fan. he is currently
working on completing a screenplay that he hopes to see made. as well
as putting together his first graphic novel. You can learn more about his
work at Ronbeekiii.com or follow him @ronbeekiiiart on Instagram.

And for any brave souls that want to get more insight into the
machinations of his clearly deranged mind (as well as those of your
author Kayla Kennedy. and our friends Ryan Alves and John Callahan)
check out "The WTFAWTA Podcast".

Lightning Source UK Ltd.
Milton Keynes UK
UKHW021709050122
396645UK00006B/70